MERCY
MOMENTS

40 DAYS
TO REKINDLE
YOUR PASSION
FOR GOD

BRIAN KINSEY

www.BrianKinsey.com

Dust Jacket Press
P.O. Box 721243
Oklahoma City, OK 73172
www.dustjacket.com

Ordering information for print editions:
Quantity sales. Special discounts are available on quantity purchases by corporations, associations, and others. For details, check out www.BrianKinsey.com.

All Scripture quotations are taken from the King James Version of the Bible.

Cover & interior design: D.E. West—www.zaqdesigns.com & Dust Jacket Creative Services

Printed in the United States of America

www.BrianKinsey.com

DEDICATION

To all who hunger to create an unbreakable
bond with the Almighty, desiring to draw closer to Him
and to mirror the magnificence of His person.

CONTENTS

INVITATION

Welcome, friend. I invite you to embark on an incredible journey with me in which we will discover the divine moments of mercy that shape us into the people God wants us to be. Daily communion with God, illuminated by His grace and a diet of the Word, will cause our hearts to flourish. I fervently hope these pages will set your heart ablaze and propel you into *your* prophetic future.

This daily journal serves as a guide to embracing the wonder of His mercy. To fully benefit from this experience, join me for the next forty days. This commitment will help solidify the habit of seeking God's mercy through Scripture, prayer, and action. Should you miss a day, do not lose heart. Simply resume from where you left off, continuing until the hunger for God's presence is kindled within you.

With steadfast faith and boundless hope, let us step into this magnificent redemption story, rediscovering His eternal mercy and love.

With unending gratitude,
Brian Kinsey

HOW TO BEGIN

This book is not a mere collection of daily reflections but rather a testament to the transformative power of God's mercy and the victories that await us when we welcome His divine presence.

As you delve into these pages, recognize that the challenges you encounter, both spiritual and material, are not insurmountable. Like the biblical hero Samson, who faced daunting lions in his quest, you too may face adversities—opposition from your spiritual foes, resistance from those hostile to God's plan for you, and your own frailties. Yet, fear not, for the strength bestowed upon you through the baptism of the Holy Ghost surpasses any obstacle.

THE PURPOSE OF THE JOURNEY

This book is a compilation of mercy moments—brief, potent opportunities to awaken your spirit to God's presence and power in your life, which the enemy seeks to conceal. Through these daily encounters you will grasp a profound truth: your victory is already secured through Christ's sacrifice at Calvary, granting you the authority to overcome any hurdle.

Step by step, this guide will lead you to where God's mercy will safeguard you from the enemy, who prowls like a roaring lion, and you will experience spiritual victory. You will realize that you are not battling alone. And you will learn to embrace God's mercy as your strength and shield.

HOW TO ENGAGE

Use this book as your daily companion. Choose a specific time each day for your mercy moment—perhaps with your morning coffee, a pause in your workday, or a quiet evening moment. Establishing a daily ritual will deepen your connection with God, enriching your life's journey.

The duration of your daily practice is personal; some may spend about ten minutes, while others might dedicate an hour to reading, prayer, and reflection. The key is consistency, making this exercise a cherished part of your day.

WHAT TO DO

During your mercy moment slow down, clear distractions, and immerse yourself in this book. Reward your dedication with something enjoyable, making this time a daily highlight.

Each mercy moment consists of four parts, which are vital for spiritual growth.

Scripture. Start with the Bible verse, allowing its words to resonate deeply. Ask for the Holy Ghost's guidance to uncover its meaning.

Word of Inspiration. Reflect on a scriptural truth, opening your heart to God's mercy in your life.

Mercy Principle. Summarize each day's insight. Consider memorizing these principles to fortify your resolve to seek God's prophetic future for your life.

Mercy in Action. Conclude by identifying an intention for a specific, actionable step in response to the day's lesson, encapsulated in brief statements:

I know. Write your discovery.

I pray. Write a prayer for yourself or others based on what you now know.

I will. Write one specific thing you can do to put truth into action. To help you identify an action, each mercy moment includes a prompt such as "Each time you start your car today, ask God to protect you wherever you go" or "Today call or email one person to thank him or her for providing accountability in your life."

THE SURE MERCIES

This forty-day journey through God's sure mercies will reveal His character and the depth of His mercy—unchanging, abundant, and available to all.

The sure mercies are presented as four legs of your journey, but you may experience them out of sequence or sometimes all at once.

Generational Mercy. The mercy of God lasts for all generations. The mercy shown to Abraham, Isaac, and Jacob is the same mercy shown to Peter, Paul, and John, and it is the same mercy that is available to you. By remaining faithful, you witness God's mercy flowing through time— blessing past, present, and future generations.

Everlasting Mercy. God's mercy is eternal. Growing in faith and obedience unveils the boundless depth of God's mercy, a divine experience that enriches your life now and forever. The wonders of God's presence and grace have no end.

Abundant Mercy. God is a God of abundance. His mercy is unfettered by time, material, or any other limitation. No sin is too deep for His mercy to forgive; no person is too lost for His mercy to find; no problem is too immense for His mercy to solve.

Enduring Mercy. God's mercy is unwavering and accessible in every circumstance. No situation can sever the bond of God's mercy—from the confines of a prison to the comfort of your home. His mercy meets your material and spiritual needs. The relationship you share with God stands as the most durable relationship in your life.

Upon completing this forty-day journey, continue cultivating the habit of seeking daily communion with God. By engaging with the Bible, reflecting on its meaning, and applying its truth, you foster a life enriched by mercy moments. This practice will be a blessing to you throughout your lifetime.

Let's begin.

GENERATIONAL MERCY

The mercy of God lasts for all generations.

The mercy shown to Abraham, Isaac, and Jacob is the same mercy shown to Peter, Paul, and John, and it is the same mercy that is available to you. By remaining faithful, you witness God's mercy flowing through time— blessing past, present, and future generations.

DAY 1

Qualified for Your Anointing

*Verily, verily, I say unto you, He that believeth
on me, the works that I do shall he do also;
and greater works than these shall he do;
because I go unto my Father.*
—John 14:12

ave you ever wondered why you don't witness miracles? Why does it seem that other people experience divine intervention in their lives frequently—but you do not? If the miracles in the Bible are true, why don't we see more of them today?

The reason we often fail to witness miracles in our lives is not due to a lack of biblical precedence; indeed, God often intervenes in human affairs in miraculous ways. The reason we fail to see and experience them can lie in our own perceptions of worthiness; we mistakenly believe that only those with a special calling or an extraordinary anointing are recipients of God's miraculous deeds. That is not the case. Through faith in Jesus Christ, you are already qualified for this anointing. You are eligible for anointing, and you are poised for miracles.

Miracles manifest through God's power, not our power or worthiness. Through your faith in Him, Jesus has qualified you to share in the inheritance of the saints. His anointing and presence are triumphantly present in you—right here, right now. There's no further qualification needed; your faith alone makes you acceptable to God.

With that in mind, live expectantly, casting aside doubts and Satan's claims of unworthiness. You are worthy because Jesus Christ made you worthy. Every generational curse is now rendered powerless by the incorruptible Word of God, which will bring every promise and power of redemption to fruition. So lift your head, square your shoulders, and walk with a backbone as strong as a sawlog. Live your life as if you are worthy of being called a child of God. You are!

Engage actively in your faith—pray, fast, profess your belief, confess and repent of sins, and hold fast to God's promises. Persistence, patience, and perseverance are key. Never lose sight of God's eternal plan and His active engagement in your life.

God is working right now. You are neither defeated nor bound by despair or discouragement. With God on your side, victory is assured. Living right and tapping into His power opens the door to experiencing His might, even to the point of witnessing miracles.

MERCY PRINCIPLE

You are already qualified to receive God's blessings.

MERCY IN ACTION

Reflect *on what God has taught you today.*
I know

Express *your commitment, desire, or request to the Lord.*
I pray

Identify a *simple act of obedience God has prompted for you today.*
I will

DAY 2

And the Father Will Dance

The Lord thy God in the midst of thee is mighty;
he will save, he will rejoice over thee with joy;
he will rest in his love,
he will joy over thee with singing.
—Zephaniah 3:17

Our understanding of joy stems from three Hebrew words, each offering a unique nuance. *Rejoicing* is derived from *sis*, suggesting pure enjoyment or great mirth. *Joy* relates to the Hebrew term *sameach*, portraying a brilliant inner light and exuberant merriment. Another biblical term, *gil*, signifies joy through dancing, spinning, and leaping with an overwhelming surge of sincere emotion.

Interestingly, today's scripture highlights not the church's dance but God's. It is the Almighty who takes to the dance floor in this splendid scene. It poses the question "What makes God dance?" The answer is beautiful: God's dance is in response to the church's realization of her rightful place, the promises bestowed upon her, and her unyielding authority. When the church fully embraces the indwelling of Jesus Christ, God's joyous dance begins, for He delights most when the church awakens to the profound reality of her sonship.

While angels rejoice at a sinner's repentance, the Lord reserves His utmost joy for the times the church asserts its dominion over the enemy. This divine dance is set in motion when we understand and live out our position in Christ Jesus, claiming our covenant privileges.

Paul tells us, "The manifestation of the Spirit is given to every man to profit withal" (1 Corinthians 12:7). *Manifestation*, from the Greek *phanerosis*, means expressing oneself publicly. From this root comes the Latin word *phalange*. Taken together, this gives us the image of the dancing hand of God—as if God is the symphony conductor of the church's worship, His hand dancing with joy as the people of God live out their true purpose with joy and love.

Envision the Father's joy as His children grow in the knowledge of truth, serve one another with their gifts, and unite in love. Just as no earthly father's joy surpasses seeing his children healthy, thriving, and mature, so our heavenly Father rejoices—even dances!—when the church flourishes, takes dominion, and transforms the world.

By embracing our identity as God's people, we ignite a dance of revelation in our hearts, joining the divine symphony orchestrated by God Himself. We become vessels of His joy, transforming lives and bringing forth abundant blessings.

MERCY PRINCIPLE

The Father's greatest delight is witnessing His children embody their role as the people of God in the world.

MERCY IN ACTION

Reflect *on what God has taught you today.*
I know

Express *your commitment, desire, or request to the Lord.*
I pray

Identify a *simple act of obedience God has prompted for you today.*
I will

DAY 3

Then Abram Removed His Tent

Then Abram removed his tent.
—Genesis 13:18

Many people find solace in being rooted in a particular place, a sentiment that may increase with age. Youthful wanderlust gradually gives way to a quest for stability, especially when starting a family. In later years the comfort of familiar surroundings, people, and routines takes precedence. History echoes this pattern. The young embark on adventures while the elderly share tales by the fireside.

That makes it all the more meaningful that Abraham took on a nomadic existence late in life. He left his home in Ur at age seventy-five and kept moving. Throughout his life, Abraham obeyed every instruction given to him, even when that meant literally moving his home—a tent. This great hero of the faith was willing to face the uncertainties and upheavals of constant relocation in obedience to God. And God blessed him abundantly.

God's guidance and sometimes His correction may require us to leave behind our comforts. Embracing God's promises involves action and movement toward fulfillment, necessitating a departure from our present circumstances. This journey can be challenging, but remember this: God's blessing and authority provide true comfort and security, which follow us wherever we go in His will. God's faithfulness ensures the realization of His promises.

Though initially challenging, transitions under God's direction bring renewal and progress from one blessing to the next. After engaging in battles with enemies and even fellow believers in the church, a season of spiritual rejuvenation becomes essential. It affirms our choices, deepens our respect for God, and reinvigorates our dedication and enthusiasm for His will.

But be careful. It's easy to mistake our desires or reasoning for God's voice. Staying connected with God through Scripture, prayer, and worship helps us recognize when He is truly instructing us to "remove our tents."

God desires that we reach our full potential as His children, motivating us to move forward. Like Abraham, we may need to figuratively or literally leave our current place to build an altar to the Lord in a new setting.

Oswald Chambers insightfully observed, "Faith never knows where it is being led, but it loves and knows the One who is leading."

MERCY PRINCIPLE

Following God sets our lives in motion.

MERCY IN ACTION

Reflect *on what God has taught you today.*
I know

Express *your commitment, desire, or request to the Lord.*
I pray

Identify a *simple act of obedience God has prompted*
for you today.
I will

DAY 4

We Are Designed for Victory

*They go from strength to strength, every one of
them in Zion appeareth before God.*
—Psalm 84:7

In the whirlwind of daily life, filled with a flurry of tasks,
obligations, messages, and requests, the pace can feel
relentless, especially for those nurturing a family in which
demands seem to multiply. It feels like running on a tread-
mill—exhausting without forward progress. This routine
can sometimes make us feel as if we are transitioning from
strength to weakness, each day starting with our feeling a
little more tired and discouraged than the day before.

When that happens, physical exhaustion is just one of
the problems we face. The more important side effect is
the weakening of our relationship with God. Busyness and
stress are the enemy's prime strategies for pulling your at-
tention away from the Lord.

God's design has always been that we grow stronger
every day, not weaker. While simplifying life through prac-

tical steps like decluttering schedules, ensuring adequate rest, or minimizing digital interruptions can provide temporary relief, these measures alone cannot reverse the downward spiral in our spiritual lives. Revitalizing our bond with God demands deliberate daily engagement with the divine.

Engaging daily with God fosters resilience amidst adversity. Pursuing God is simpler than it may seem. It starts with being open to His presence—pausing the hustle to be still, attuning ourselves to the Spirit, and listening for His voice. What does His voice sound like? Most often it's a gentle prompting in your heart and mind, pointing you to some truth or action. Scripture reading and prayer are invaluable aids in developing this relationship.

In choosing to pursue God, we find the strength to move forward, assured of His enduring provision of grace for our journey. Every hardship we face is met with abundant grace, empowering not just survival but also growth. Conversely, neglecting to pursue God and focusing instead on our daily turmoil leads to a decline in spiritual strength—and the cycle of stress, anxiety, and distance from God gains momentum.

Seek God today. If you have taken a step back in your faith, don't despair. Seize this chance to recommit yourself to Him and strengthen your relationship with Him. Your dedication to the Lord, marked by regular communion with Him, will remind you of His grace, love, and mercy. Armed with the Lord's strength and faith in your heart, you will progress from strength to strength and appear before Him with a pure heart and faithful spirit.

MERCY PRINCIPLE

We gain strength from spending time with God.

MERCY IN ACTION

Reflect *on what God has taught you today.*
I know

Express *your commitment, desire, or request to the Lord.*
I pray

Identify a *simple act of obedience God has prompted for you today.*
I will

DAY 5

The Blessing of Asher

*And of Asher he said, Let Asher be
blessed with children; let him be acceptable to
his brethren, and let him dip his foot in oil.
Thy shoes shall be iron and brass; and as
thy days, so shall thy strength be.*
—Deuteronomy 33:24–25

Moses pronounced a blessing over Asher that was rich in promise. Asher was the eighth son of Jacob, so it is interesting that he was given the blessing of abundance, favor, and strength. Asher's birth marked the end of a time of barrenness for Leah. She had given Jacob four sons but then ceased bearing. When Asher was born to Zilpah, her handmaid, Leah said, "Happy am I, for the daughters will call me blessed: and she called his name   Asher" (Genesis 30:13). Asher's name means "happy" or "blessed." Though less loved than Rachel, Leah made up her mind to be happy. Then God opened her womb, and she bore three more children.

In the larger context of the biblical story, the birth of Asher symbolizes God's unwavering faithfulness and determination to bless His children with abundance. No matter the present circumstances, God's promise of abundance remains in effect. Here are some of the ways God wants to bless you:

Favor. His children were selected to produce oil for the sanctuary, which benefited all of God's people, placing them in high status.

Abundance. The blessing of ample oil for his children, so much so that they could bathe their feet in it, represented financial prosperity.

Protection and Dominion. He was promised brass shoes, which symbolized security, peace, and authority over spiritual adversaries.

Renewal and Strength. God promised Asher's children enduring strength and an ever-transforming life to sustain them.

For those grappling with unmet expectations or unfulfilled desires, the blessing of Asher serves as a comforting reminder of God's promises. Despite past disappointments or present longings, we can take heart. We are encouraged to hold on to the assurance that God is faithful to His word. He intends to grant you the same blessings given to Asher.

MERCY PRINCIPLE

God's blessings for you exceed your imagination.

MERCY IN ACTION

Reflect *on what God has taught you today.*
I know

Express *your commitment, desire, or request to the Lord.*
I pray

Identify a *simple act of obedience God has prompted for you today.*
I will

DAY 6

On Waiting

*And therefore will the Lord wait,
that he may be gracious unto you, and therefore will he be exalted, that he may have mercy
upon you: for the Lord is a God of judgment:
blessed are all they that wait for him.*
—Isaiah 30:18

No one likes to be kept waiting, but sometimes it's good for us. That may be why God so often delays answering our prayers, either with a yes or a no. God's timing frequently includes periods of waiting, as illustrated throughout the Bible. Jacob, for instance, sought God's blessing his entire life. Finally, after a night-long struggle with an angel, he begged for, even demanded, the blessing of God—and it was given. The apostle Paul asked the Lord three times to remove a "thorn in the flesh." Finally, after months, perhaps even years, of waiting, Paul got his answer: no. Instead of relief, Paul received the promise that God's grace was sufficient for him.

This principle of divine delay is one of the hardest lessons for a believer to understand. It's frustrating and painful to be left in the dark. But God's reasons for making us wait are always rooted in His wisdom, designed to teach us valuable lessons.

One such lesson is recognizing God's sovereignty in giving and withholding, trusting that His actions are always for our benefit. Often we ask for things too lightly, expecting a quick fix to our problems. Delays can heighten our desires, prompting us to reflect on our motives and whether we seek God's best. The more we yearn for God's gift, the more we will value it when it is given.

Waiting also corrects misconceptions, revealing our total dependence on God rather than viewing Him as a mere aide to our plans. The longer we wait for God's help, the more we see how greatly we need it. These times of waiting shift our perspective from God as a helper for our endeavors to that of the sovereign ruler of our lives.

These realizations, though humbling, are *mercy moments,* providing clarity about our limitations in light of God's omnipotence. They may help you see that you have been working for God based on your own wisdom, expecting Him to come along and bless what you've chosen to do. Such moments of insight, often encountered during waiting periods, are pivotal for faith development and life transformation.

As you experience God's timing, you will begin to value these intervals of revelation, approaching periods of waiting with less anxiety and more trust in God's perfect timing and answers.

MERCY PRINCIPLE

Waiting on God brings us closer to Him.

MERCY IN ACTION

Reflect *on what God has taught you today.*
I know

Express *your commitment, desire, or request to the Lord.*
I pray

Identify *a step to maintain patience and faithfulness as you await God's response.*
I will

DAY 7

The "Next To" Anointing

But the Comforter, which is
the Holy Ghost, whom the Father will send in
my name, he shall teach you all things,
and bring all things to your remembrance,
whatsoever I have said unto you.
—John 14:26

Anyone who has studied the science of time management or productivity management knows the power of the word *next*. This seemingly simple term enhances focus by grouping similar tasks—a principle known as proximity. Moreover, it bolsters project momentum by clearly identifying the immediately following step—a principle known as *sequencing*. These principles parallel our spiritual lives, emphasizing the importance of being "next to" our spiritual support systems and continuously seeking the next step in our walk with God.

The "next to" concept reminds us to align ourselves with spiritual mentors and communities. Just as in time management, in which the next action is crucial for maintaining flow and productivity, being "next to" individuals who provide spiritual support and guidance can significantly impact our growth and resilience in our spiritual journey. Consider the influence of your closest relationships. Aligning with those who pursue a deeper relationship with God can inspire and uplift us, whereas the opposite can lead to spiritual decline. It has been said that you are the sum of the five people who are closest to you in relationships. Surrounding yourself with individuals committed to seeking God's will can catalyze your own spiritual development.

Additionally, the concept of "next" encourages believers to strive for the next anointing by continually seeking God's direction for our lives and the blessings He is eager to give us. Our journey toward spiritual maturity is ongoing, aiming for the likeness of Christ. Complacency or the belief that we've reached spiritual completion is a deviation from this goal. There is always a subsequent level of anointing to pursue. Seek it, and God will lead you to it.

Remember the words of Jesus just before His departure. He said it was important for Him to return to the Father because that would allow the Comforter to come. Who is the Comforter? It is the Holy Ghost, who comes inside us, walks next to us, and leads us into all truth.

By aligning with like-minded individuals, inviting the Holy Ghost's guidance, and pursuing continual growth, we navigate the path of mercy and transformation.

MERCY PRINCIPLE

Your character is shaped by those closest to you.

MERCY IN ACTION

Reflect *on what God has taught you today.*
I know

Express *your commitment, desire, or request to the Lord.*
I pray

Identify a *simple act of obedience God has prompted for you today.*
I will

DAY 8

Who Also Will Do It

Faithful is he that calleth you,
who also will do it.
—1 Thessalonians 5:24

Owning an old or malfunctioning vehicle can instill a unique type of anxiety. You know the feeling you get when you turn the key and the motor cranks and cranks but doesn't fire. Or when you've been driving for a while and the engine starts sputtering—and you remember your gas gauge is broken. Or when the vehicle decelerates instead of accelerating uphill. There ought to be a name for that sick feeling you get when you realize the old clunker is about to leave you stranded.

Similarly, this apprehension can surface in our relationship with God, especially during tumultuous times. Whether one faces illness, family strife, or global crises, it's tempting to question God's capacity to guide us through.

The Bible lists countless examples of God's faithfulness to His people, even in the most difficult circumstances.

Consider Abraham, who doubted the fulfillment of God's promise of a son due to seemingly insurmountable odds—yet God delivered. The Israelites' journey from slavery to the promised land led through the desert, and they wondered if God would take them all the way home. He did. Time and again, God proved His faithfulness. His promises never fail. He is the same yesterday, today, and forever.

God's faithfulness is intrinsic to His character. The Psalms declare, "For His merciful kindness is great toward us: and the truth of the Lord endureth forever. Praise ye the Lord" (117:2). Paul emphasizes that even when we falter, God remains steadfast, unable to deny His essence (2 Timothy 2:13). Just as God is love (1 John 4:8), so too is He the embodiment of faithfulness.

In this life we are not exempt from trials or pain. The assurance of a problem-free existence awaits us in heaven; until then, we face our challenges with the knowledge that God is our steadfast support, committed to shaping us into His vision for us.

But we have a reliable vehicle to take us through this journey. God has called us, and He will ensure that we become everything He desires us to be. Those who dwell in fellowship with Christ are safeguarded by His faithfulness; He is a trustworthy keeper of His promises. Faithful is He who calls you, who also will do it.

MERCY PRINCIPLE

God's faithfulness is our anchor through life's trials.

MERCY IN ACTION

Reflect *on what God has taught you today.*
I know

Express *your commitment, desire, or request to the Lord.*
I pray

Identify *a concern you will release today, trusting in God's faithfulness.*
I will

DAY 9

The Open Heart

And a certain woman named Lydia, a seller of purple,
of the city of Thyatira, which worshipped God, heard us:
whose heart the Lord opened, that she attended unto
the things which were spoken of Paul.
—Acts 16:14

Lydia's conversion story is both intriguing and enlightening, demonstrating the ways in which God orchestrates events in our lives. God meticulously arranged the circumstances leading to Lydia's encounter with the gospel, a truth that applies to each of us.

A merchant of purple in Thyatira, Lydia found herself precisely where she needed to be to hear Paul's message at a pivotal moment. Paul's missionary journey, which had spanned numerous cities, was divinely directed to intersect with Lydia's life. Our encounters with Jesus are similarly preordained; the Spirit diligently works to align us with those who can guide us toward Him.

God had already prepared Lydia's heart for the message of salvation. As a Jew, she possessed a foundational knowledge of God, setting the stage for her introduction to Jesus. Her active seeking of God, demonstrated by her attendance at a place of prayer on the Sabbath, was met with a divine response. The Spirit's preparatory work in our hearts may manifest through questions, a conviction of sin, or humbling experiences that make us receptive to the truth.

Despite Lydia's seeking, her conversion wasn't a solitary journey. Paul's inspired words provided the necessary connection, presenting her with transformative truth. Salvation invariably involves another—the one who shares the gospel, as articulated by Paul in Romans. We can't turn to God without hearing the gospel, which can't be heard without someone to proclaim it.

Yes, Lydia had a role to play in this. She chose to respond when God prompted her. She was a seeker after God, taking steps to engage with Him and ultimately embracing Christ. However, it was God who orchestrated her salvation.

This narrative underscores a vital spiritual principle: our journey with God is initiated and sustained by Him. He prepares our hearts, orchestrates our divine encounters, and opens our minds to the gospel. While we are called to respond to His grace, the entirety of our faith journey is dependent on God.

One more thing. Lydia's life was changed by grace. She sealed her commitment to Christ through baptism and her life became a radiant example of discipleship. Just as God radically changed Lydia's life, He offers to do the same for us if we allow Him.

MERCY PRINCIPLE

We are saved by God's grace, not by our own efforts.

MERCY IN ACTION

Reflect *on what God has taught you today.*
I know

Express *your commitment, desire, or request to the Lord.*
I pray

Identify *a concern you will release today, trusting in God's faithfulness.*
I will

DAY 10

Finding God in the Darkness

And all the people saw the thunderings,
and the lightnings, and the noise of the
trumpet, and the mountain smoking:
and when the people saw it, they removed,
and stood afar off. And they said unto Moses,
Speak thou with us, and we will hear: but let
not God speak with us, lest we die. And Moses
said unto the people, Fear not: for God is come
to prove you, and that his fear may be before
your faces, that ye sin not. And the people
stood afar off, and Moses drew near unto the
thick darkness where God was.
—Exodus 20:18–21

The fear the Israelites felt as they stood before the mountain where God's presence was manifest is understandable. The signs were formidable: ear-splitting claps of thunder, lightning piercing through an unnaturally darkened sky, swiftly moving clouds resembling smoke, and a noise akin to an approaching freight train—elements reminiscent of an impending tornado. Their fear was justified, given the overwhelming nature of these manifestations.

Encountering God's majesty directly is an overwhelming experience beyond any human capacity. Yet few people come close enough to the Almighty to experience that shock and awe. Today most people fear God for different reasons. They perceive Him as harsh, cruel, vindictive, and eager to punish His children. This fear is rooted in misconceptions and false teachings, leading to a distorted view of God as a punitive force rather than understanding His true nature. No wonder they are afraid.

Moses's experience offers a deeper insight into God's character. While the people cowered in fear, Moses approached the thick darkness where God resided. At that moment God revealed a specific place to Moses by His side, a spot where Moses could stand and witness God's glory without being consumed by it. In this sacred proximity, Moses conversed with God as one would with a close friend. This is the relationship that Jesus later likened to the relationship between a child and his or her father. Though God is all-powerful, there is no reason for His children to fear His presence. Moses knew he did not have to fear the darkness—he could approach it with the confidence that God rules even in the darkness.

To truly know God, we must be willing to overcome our fear and draw near to Him. We must learn to hear His voice and to distinguish that voice from the misconceptions spread by others. Just as Moses found his place at

God's side, we too can find our spiritual refuge, a place to listen to His guiding words. God's words bring hope, affirming the existence of a personal space for each of us to connect with Him intimately.

Moses's bravery in approaching God encourages us to face the divine with openness. God desires to refine us and lead us away from sin, instilling reverence and awe in His presence. He understands our human nature and meets with unconditional grace our genuine efforts to connect with Him. God's words to us are not reprimands but rather expressions of love intended to guide and strengthen us on our journey.

Life is filled with distractions and challenges, requiring us to focus and attune ourselves to God's voice. While God's grandeur may be too overwhelming for us to behold, He communicates in a gentle whisper. We can deepen our understanding of Him by listening to this subtle voice.

MERCY PRINCIPLE

To know God we must draw near to Him.

MERCY IN ACTION

Reflect *on what God has taught you today.*
I know

Express *your commitment, desire, or request to the Lord.*
I pray

Identify a *simple act of obedience God has prompted for you today.*
I will

EVERLASTING MERCY

God's mercy is eternal.

Growing in faith and obedience unveils the boundless depth of God's mercy, a divine experience that enriches your life now and forever. The wonders of God's presence and grace have no end.

DAY 11

Wake Up the Wind

Awake, O north wind; and come, thou south;
blow upon my garden, that the spices thereof
may flow out. Let my beloved come into his
garden, and eat his pleasant fruits.
—Song of Solomon 4:16

The world began in a garden and all of Scripture speaks of its return. Eden was destroyed by the sin of the first man, Adam. Our return to a better world is made possible by Jesus, the second Adam. This divine re-creation begins here, now, on earth and will be completed later, throughout eternity, in heaven.

Solomon, the philosopher-king of Israel, describes this fulfillment in allegorical terms in his poetic work known as Song of Solomon. The speaker calls upon winds from all directions to awaken her garden, representing the potential growth in each of us that waits to be realized. The garden signifies our lives. Our dreams and aspirations may have been dormant for many years, perhaps a lifetime. Yet through the breath of God we can be revived and reawakened to a new life filled with promise.

First comes the north wind. Cold, even brutal, it can also be refreshing. The north wind symbolizes our need to turn toward God and take action based on faith. This frigid blast awakens the spirit within us, forces us to abandon complacency, and drives us to make changes. The promises of God are real and trustworthy, even if we have not yet seen them fulfilled. The north wind encourages us to move forward step by step, trusting in God and His plan. Through faith we have the confidence to believe that a lush garden will bloom in what now appears to be the barren landscape of our lives.

Next comes the south wind, which signifies power. Whereas the north wind rouses and destroys, forcing movement, the south wind can be harnessed. This is the wind that propels sailing ships around the world and drives windmills, generating power for useful industries. The south wind signifies the power we receive when we claim the promises of God. These promises are not empty words. God has promised us power through the Holy Spirit and we can confidently stake our claim in them. As we embrace these promises, we experience the power and abundance He provides to transform our lives and to serve Him in the world.

The east wind represents the importance of praise and gratitude. Just as the standard of the camp of Judah was positioned facing the rising sun, we must direct our hearts toward God, warming our souls through praise and worship. When we face the east wind, we allow the light of hope and assurance to shine brightly within us, dispelling any darkness that may hinder our progress. This is the blessing that comes from maintaining an attitude of thankfulness.

The west wind represents the fulfillment of all that God intends for us. It encourages us not to settle for mere blessings but rather to seek the complete fulfillment of God's purpose for our lives. Just as the west side of Jordan was the true promised land, we are encouraged to go after all that God has in store for us, wholeheartedly embracing His plans and blessings.

Powered by the wind of the Spirit, we can cultivate a thriving garden of purpose and fulfillment in our lives. Turn to the promises of God. Claim them by faith. Praise Him with gratitude for what He has done. And seek the fulfillment of His purpose in your life and in the world.

MERCY PRINCIPLE

God will fulfill His purpose in you.

MERCY IN ACTION

Reflect *on what God has taught you today.*
I know

Express *your commitment, desire, or request to the Lord.*
I pray

Identify a *simple act of obedience God has prompted
for you today.*
I will

DAY 12

One Thing I Have Desired

*And thou saidst, I will surely do thee good, and
make thy seed as the sand of the sea, which
cannot be numbered for multitude.*
—Genesis 32:12

When Jacob made up his mind to return to Canaan, he found himself separated from his brother Esau by a stream. Esau, accompanied by armed men, was on the opposite side. The last time the two had met, Esau had sworn to kill Jacob. Not knowing what the morning might bring, Jacob fervently sought God's protection, reminding Him, "And thou saidst, I will surely do thee good."

This prayer referenced the covenant God had made with Abraham, Jacob's grandfather, promising to make his descendants as numerous as the sands and to bless all nations through him. God had said that Abraham's descendants would become as numerous as the sands on the seashore and that the entire world would be blessed through him. Now, two generations later, Jacob boldly reminded God of His promise, asserting, "You must help me because you promised."

God's faithfulness stands as a pillar of His character, a firm foundation we can rely on. His word is unfailing. What He has promised He will fulfill. As Paul wrote to the church in Rome, "Let God be true, but every man a liar" (Romans 3:4). God's promises remain steadfast and will be fully realized.

Jacob may have been the first to remind God of His promises, but he was not the last. Solomon, during the temple dedication, employed this same powerful plea. He invoked God's promise to his father, David, and implored Him to bless that sacred place. The psalmists also frequently call on God to "remember" His promises.

God's promises are like bearer bonds, redeemable by whoever holds them. If a financial institution were to default on even one promissory note, the entire organization would collapse. If God were to renege on a promise, it would undermine His deity. Yet His integrity is unassailable, His timing impeccable, always neither early nor late.

A study of God's Word alongside the experiences of His people reveals a consistent fulfillment of His promises. Joshua attested, "Not one thing hath failed of all the good things which the Lord your God spake concerning you; all are come to pass" (Joshua 23:14).

Possessing a divine promise means you can claim it with confidence. The Lord intended to fulfill the promise. Otherwise, He would not have given it. God does not offer hollow assurances or temporary consolation. His promises are commitments to action. When God speaks, it signifies His intention to fulfill.

MERCY PRINCIPLE

God's promises cannot fail.

MERCY IN ACTION

Reflect *on what God has taught you about His faithfulness.*
I know

Express *a specific promise from God for which you seek fulfillment.*
I pray

Identify a *simple act of obedience God has prompted for you today.*
I will

DAY 13

The Value of a Foundation

*O thou afflicted, tossed with tempest,
and not comforted, behold, I will lay thy
stones with fair colours, and lay thy
foundations with sapphires.*
—Isaiah 54:11

Sapphires, among the most exquisite gems created by God, are also incredibly durable, second only to diamonds in hardness. Their brilliant blue hue captures and reflects light in a mesmerizing manner. A foundation built upon sapphires would captivate with its beauty and stand impregnable.

This is the foundation God establishes for us, but we seldom perceive its value. Our relationship with God is anchored in the unseen. These hidden foundations reveal what is truly valuable and precious in our journey with Him. Everything God does for us, through us, and in us is priceless.

Proverbs imparts wisdom, stating, "The fear of the Lord is a fountain of life, to depart from the snares of death" (14:27). Choosing to walk with God and honor Him paves the way for a life of stability and longevity. Grounded in the truth of God's Word, we find the strength to withstand life's trials and temptations.

How can we ensure that our foundation remains unshakable? First, by being rooted in Scripture, absorbing and applying God's Word, not merely listening but also actively living it out. Letting the Word animate our being shapes our thoughts and actions and guides us at each stage of life's journey.

Another way to maintain this foundation is by regularly engaging with other believers through prayer, worship, fellowship, and service. As "iron sharpeneth iron" (Proverbs 27:17), the fellowship with other "precious stones" in the faith aids in our spiritual growth. The community holds us accountable, offering support during trials and temptations, thus deepening our connection with God.

Additionally, we must remain humble before the Lord. When we confess our sins and weaknesses, acknowledging our need for God, He responds with His strength. Pride blinds us to our spiritual needs and distorts our understanding of scripture, but humility removes those blinders.

Nothing can insulate you from the troubles life brings. Just as storms beat upon every house, every spiritual foundation will also be tested. Only those rooted in Jesus Christ will stand, emerging stronger from the trials.

Today, recommit to fortifying your faith's foundation. Engage with scripture through reading, meditation, and .

study. Surround yourself with brothers and sisters in Christ for mutual encouragement and accountability. Continually humble yourself before God, remaining receptive to the Spirit's guidance. Building your life on God's foundation ensures resilience against hardship or adversity, mirroring the beauty of God's salvation.

MERCY PRINCIPLE

A life founded on faith in God will endure hard times.

MERCY IN ACTION

Reflect *on what God has taught you today.*
I know

Express *your commitment, desire, or request to the Lord.*
I pray

Identify a *simple act of obedience God has prompted for you today.*
I will

DAY 14

When You Can't See Clearly

*And I will make thy windows of agates,
and thy gates of carbuncles, and all thy
borders of pleasant stones.*
—Isaiah 54:12

Some buildings feature translucent windows, allowing light to pass through while obscuring specific details. This setup offers privacy but doesn't facilitate a clear view of the outside world.

Our life here on earth is a bit like living in a house with translucent windows. The church is like a building, Isaiah says. That building was designed by God, the heavenly architect. This divine construction incorporates windows— symbolizing our insight into the world beyond—crafted by God's power. But we're not in heaven yet; we're within the confines of this structure, peering through windows of agate. Agate, a translucent stone, permits light transmission but is riddled with swirls and colors, offering us a veiled glimpse of the celestial. We can see enough to perceive the magnificence of Jesus and acknowledge Him as the Lord of all, yet much remains beyond our grasp.

The apostle Paul used a metaphor similar to this in 1 Corinthians. He said, "For now we see through a glass, darkly" (13:12), alluding to our constrained and imperfect comprehension of worldly and divine matters. It's like looking at a reflection in a cloudy mirror. But we have faith that one day we will see things clearly. That's why we need faith. By faith we know that these barely perceivable things are actually real, and we are assured they will soon be revealed fully.

Our vision may be limited, but faith enables us to see beyond what we can observe with our senses. We have hope that one day we will see clearly how God has worked by grace to save us. We can know the ways in which God is working to reveal Himself to us in our present dilemmas. Eventually we will perceive all things clearly in God's presence.

Making sense of our circumstances sometimes feels almost impossible, with our understanding foggy or opaque. Yet guided by the light of the Lord Jesus Christ, we navigate this unknown path step by step. So don't be anxious, discouraged, or despairing. Don't stay stuck in the gloom. Keep moving toward the light, even if it seems dim at times. Ultimately we will be transformed into Christ's likeness, seeing Him in His true essence.

MERCY PRINCIPLE

*Our understanding of Jesus is limited now,
but it will become clear later.*

MERCY IN ACTION

Reflect *on what God has taught you today.*
I know

Express *your commitment, desire, or request to the Lord.*
I pray

Identify *an action to enhance your understanding of Jesus
today.*
I will

DAY 15

Declare the Decree of the Lord

I will declare the decree of the Lord:
the Lord hath said unto me, Thou art my Son;
this day have I begotten thee.
—Psalm 2:7

heard of a missionary whose car was unreliable. To start the car he had to push it or let it roll downhill a little way, then let out the clutch so the wheels would turn the engine over, generate a spark, and get the motor running. When a new missionary came to take his place, the fellow patiently explained the process to the newcomer. "I always try to park on a hill," he said. "That way I don't have to get someone to help me push the car." The new arrival looked under the hood and noticed the battery cable was loose. He tightened it with a screwdriver, got into the car, turned the key, and the engine roared to life.

Like that former missionary, we often bump along in our spiritual lives, making only sporadic progress. God doesn't lack the power or willingness to transform our lives; we just haven't accessed that power. As a car needs gas, oil, and spark, we need preparation, purity, and prayer in the Holy Ghost to reach a new level of spiritual power and maturity.

To access God's power, we must prepare ourselves. This involves disciplined engagement with God's Word and worship, laying the groundwork for spiritual growth. You won't catch fish if you never go fishing. And you won't grow in spirit unless you position yourself to receive God's power.

Purity is also crucial, demanding vigilance over our thoughts and words to ensure alignment with God's will. It's about heeding the Holy Ghost's guidance. Impurity often stems from entertaining thoughts and expressions that veer from God's directives. Obedience to the Holy Ghost is the cornerstone of purity.

Prayer in the Holy Ghost is also needed to increase our spiritual power. In Scripture we learn of God and feed the mind. In prayer we experience God and come to know Him personally. This strengthens our spirit and equips us for spiritual battles. Without consistent prayer, we risk languishing in spiritual mediocrity, wondering what's missing.

Our self-driven efforts to fulfill God's purpose can feel like manually pushing a car to start—inefficient and ultimately futile. By preparing our hearts, following the leading of the Spirit, and engaging in daily prayer we can unlock the realm of the Spirit and declare what God has decreed to see a fulfillment of His kingdom purpose.

MERCY PRINCIPLE

When you are not hearing from God,
check your connection with Him.

MERCY IN ACTION

Reflect *on what God has taught you today.*
I know

Express *your commitment, desire, or request to the Lord.*
I pray

Identify a *simple act of obedience God has prompted*
for you today.
I will

DAY 16

The Best Time to Pray

Offer unto God thanksgiving,
and pay thy vows unto the most High.
And call upon me in the day of trouble:
I will deliver thee, and thou shalt glorify me.
—Psalm 50:14–15

A young child who was feeling wronged after being corrected at the dinner table resolved to run away from home, hoping to teach his parents a lesson. His bemused mother helped him pack a small suitcase and even prepared a sandwich for his journey. Filled with juvenile self-righteousness, he set off down the street. However, as he ventured farther from home, doubt crept in. Where would he go? How would he get there? He didn't know. But rather than turn around and ask for help, he kept walking.

After he had gone about a block, the boy's father pulled up alongside him in the car, rolled down the window, and said, "I'm going to the store. I can give you a ride that far if you'd like." The boy got in, grateful not to be alone but still too proud to ask for help. When they reached the store, the father said, "I guess we might just as well go home. What do you think?"

"Okay," the boy said, nearly overcome with relief.

I know the child, now a grown man, who had that experience. And it illustrates a basic principle of God's mercy. When we most require God's assistance, we often find ourselves reluctant to seek it. Yet the solution to our dilemmas, self-inflicted or otherwise, lies in turning our hearts toward our spiritual home.

In adversity we might run away from God rather than toward Him. Sometimes we are angry with God, believing our problems are His doing. At other times we feel guilt. We know we've created our own mess and are too ashamed to ask for help. However, it's precisely during these times that calling upon God brings us closer to Him and glorifies Him, affirming our faith in His sovereignty and care. Calling upon God in times of trouble acknowledges His omnipotence and strengthens our faith, reinforcing our hope and belief in His goodness and mercy. This act of faith, vocalized through prayer, empowers us and reaffirms our commitment to God.

Do not allow the mistakes and setbacks of the past to disqualify you from the glorious inheritance God has prepared for you. The best time to pray is when you are in trouble. Your purpose remains, awaiting your pursuit with courage and determination. In moments of hardship, turn to God in prayer; He is listening and ready to respond.

MERCY PRINCIPLE

Draw nearer to God, not farther away.

MERCY IN ACTION

Reflect *on what God has taught you today.*
I know

Express *your commitment, desire, or request to the Lord.*
I pray

Identify a *simple act of obedience God has prompted for you today.*
I will

DAY 17

Perfect That Which Concerneth Me

The Lord will perfect that which concerneth me:
thy mercy, O Lord, endureth forever: forsake not
the works of thine own hands.
—Psalm 138:8

Self-confidence is a much-desired trait. Some seem to be bursting with it. Athletes, for example, boldly predict the outcome of an upcoming game, always in their favor. Politicians claim they will reshape the state of the nation. However, such confidence often rests on uncertain foundations—ourselves. Confidence is only as reliable as its object.

In the Scriptures, King David exemplified true confidence. He predicted he would defeat the giant Goliath. He had no fear in opposing King Saul and later doing battle with the enemies of Israel. The man oozed confidence. But it was not confidence in his own abilities—his confidence and his victories stemmed from his unwavering trust in the Lord.

Asserting that God will complete what concerns us reflects our faith in His promises, understanding that the outcome depends on God's fidelity, not our capabilities. If we make claims based on our plans, intellect, or ability, we're likely to be disappointed—and to disappoint others. Our declarations should align with trust in God's Word, acknowledging His faithfulness.

Self-affirmations are a popular form of empowerment today. It is thought that by repeating positive statements such as "I can do whatever I choose," "I am strong and powerful," or "I will succeed at whatever I attempt," we can turn our dreams into reality. While self-affirmations can sometimes motivate, they fall short of guaranteeing success.

True confidence and peace arise from acknowledging our limitations and God's omnipotence. Our achievements highlight our sufficiency in God's power and faithfulness. Ultimately our trust must reside not in ourselves but in God.

That level of trust in God necessitates complete surrender to His will, including obedience to His Word and purification from sin. Pretending to trust God for our overarching welfare while disregarding Him in daily decisions reveals a lack of genuine faith.

David beautifully expressed his unwavering faith in God's perfecting power. He truly believed the Lord would bring to completion everything that pertained to his life. Like David, we can rest assured in God's commitment to see every aspect of our lives to completion when we place our trust wholly in Him.

MERCY PRINCIPLE

Even when you can't trust yourself,
you can always count on God.

MERCY IN ACTION

Reflect *on what God has taught you today.*
I know

Express *your commitment, desire, or request to the Lord.*
I pray

Identify a *simple act of obedience God has prompted*
for you today.
I will

DAY 18

You Have Been Chosen

My sons, be not now negligent:
for the Lord hath chosen you to stand before
him, to serve him, and that ye should minister
unto him, and burn incense.
—2 Chronicles 29:11

Hezekiah, king of Judah, was a reformer who implemented various measures to purge corruption and restore genuine worship of God. His initiatives included repairing the temple, encouraging Passover observance, and consecrating priests.

One of the most compelling aspects of Hezekiah's leadership was his approach to guiding priests. He used a particularly poignant phrase when directing their consecration and service, referring to them as "my sons." These simple words were loaded with meaning—a term of endearment and respect, signifying a profound transformation. Through royal recognition, ordinary individuals were elevated to an esteemed status, imbued with the authority and responsibility to serve with distinction.

This narrative mirrors a powerful declaration found in the gospel of John: "But as many as received him, to them gave he power to become the sons of God, even to them that believe on his name" (John 1:12). Embracing our role as God's children facilitates a direct and enduring connection, granting access to divine power that shapes our identity and purpose. By allowing God to fill the void in our lives, we step into our calling with conviction and strength.

Acknowledging our identity as sons and daughters of the King affirms our value and significance and compels us to honor the duties and gifts entrusted to us by our heavenly Father. Just as the priests were instructed not to neglect their duty, we are encouraged not to overlook the responsibilities and gifts bestowed upon us by our heavenly Father. This obedient stance deepens our intimacy with God, enabling His transformative work within and through us.

As God's children we are granted direct access to the divine realm, where transformative power abides. This connection enables us to overcome challenges and mature into the individuals God intended us to be. Liberated from the pursuit of worldly satisfaction, we find wholeness in God's presence. We can fully embrace our identity and walk in the fullness of our calling, guided by the love of our heavenly King.

You are a cherished son or daughter of the King, chosen to stand in His presence, serve Him, and offer prayers as incense. Do not neglect your calling, but embrace it with confidence and joy, for your heavenly Father deeply loves and values you. Allow God to work in your life to unveil a transformative power that infuses every step of your journey with hope, validation, and purpose.

MERCY PRINCIPLE

*Embracing your identity empowers
you to fulfill your calling.*

MERCY IN ACTION

Reflect *on what God has taught you today.*
I know

Express *your commitment, desire, or request to the Lord.*
I pray

Identify a *simple act of obedience God has prompted
for you today.*
I will

DAY 19

Trained to Be Void of Offense

And herein do I exercise myself,
to have always a conscience void of offence
toward God, and toward men.
—Acts 24:16

Paul met many offenses along the path of divine purpose in his journey of faith. His obedience to the heavenly vision did not exempt him from these offenses, but his choice to live above them has become a model of devotion to Jesus Himself that we should follow today. It was his desire to endeavor to maintain a conscience "void of offence toward God, and toward men." This discipline is like that of an athlete who trains diligently to condition himself for victory. But in Paul's case, it involved aligning himself to the will of God.

Paul knew he had a tendency to become offended and bitter, just like everyone else. But he was determined to become everything God wanted him to be. So he immersed himself in the purpose of God for his life and the church he desired to advance on the earth. Dedicated to the cross of Jesus Christ, he filtered all his actions through the lens of what brought glory to God, not himself. Not only is this God's will for all of us, but also God is committed to helping us accomplish this magnificent feat—to be "void of offense."

God designed His kingdom so we would each be influenced by our *conscience,* which means "co-perceiver." The Holy Ghost influences our minds to accept a divine perspective. To be "void of offense" means relinquishing our right to ourselves and never using our anointing to retaliate or seek vengeance. It is a divine invitation to become like Jesus and respond with forgiveness and a ministry of reconciliation. This divine perception enables us to triumph over adversity—not by might nor by power, but by the Spirit of the Lord (Zechariah 4:6).

As followers of Christ, we need to commit daily to immersing our minds in the Word of God. For it is the Word that overthrows wrong thinking, renews our minds, and equips us to live unoffended in a world filled with offense.

Today, may you embrace this divine training, holding fast to a clean conscience that is washed in the blood, led by the Spirit, and obedient to the Word of God. We can now walk in peace; we now are testimonies of the keeping power of God, declaring His enduring mercy to all generations.

MERCY PRINCIPLE

God is for you, not against you.

MERCY IN ACTION

Reflect *on what God has taught you today.*
I know

Express *your commitment, desire, or request to the Lord.*
I pray

Identify a *simple act of obedience God has prompted for you today.*
I will

DAY 20

Walk Before Me

Walk before me, and be thou perfect.
—Genesis 17:1

Most people procrastinate once in a while, and some have become masters of the art. As one fellow humorously remarked, "I don't like wasting time. I'm just good at it." Another quipped, "I'm not a procrastinator. I'm just extremely productive at unimportant things."

This sentiment resonates with many. No student feels more motivated to clean his or her room than when a term paper is due. And plenty of dads develop a sudden urge to reorganize the garage when it's time to file income taxes. It's not that we are unaware of which tasks are essential or lack the desire to complete them. Rather, the most significant and demanding tasks intimidate us, causing us to shy away from them.

Yet as has been aptly stated, "Procrastination is like a credit card. It's a lot of fun until you get the bill." There is invariably a cost to delaying important tasks, be it a lower grade, a late fee, or the guilt of not doing what we ought to have done.

Spiritual procrastination operates on a similar principle. God often calls us to undertake important and challenging things that require significant effort. The challenge isn't in our reluctance but in the difficulty of starting. And this delay is costly.

Whenever the Lord makes a promise, He expects us to act and move toward it. Our current circumstances often seem more comfortable than the unknown future. That must have been true for Abram when God instructed him to pick up and move.

God's promises to Abram were vast: numerous blessings, countless descendants, and a spiritual heritage that would bless the entire world. But to access these blessings, Abram had to take action. He needed to move. When Abram moved, God moved with him. Abram didn't procrastinate; he obeyed God and the promise was secured by his actions. Similarly, we may need to pry ourselves loose and set on a journey to be faithful to God's call. While daunting, acting on our dreams and aspirations opens us up to receive the abundance that God has promised. The truth is that many times God will not act until we do. When God sees us move, then He moves into action. Otherwise, the promise lays dormant.

Procrastinators miss out on one crucial experience— the thrill of achievement. Procrastination yields only the stress of impending deadlines. In contrast, confronting and accomplishing a challenging task brings satisfaction and joy in our achievements.

Abram was able to offer a sacrifice to God, thankful for His direction and for the courage to act upon it. By responding to God's call and acting on His will, you too can build an altar of praise for the ways He has blessed you.

MERCY PRINCIPLE

Faithfulness requires action.

MERCY IN ACTION

Reflect *on what God has taught you today.*
I know

Express *your commitment, desire, or request to the Lord.*
I pray

Identify a *simple act of obedience God has prompted for you today.*
I will

ABUNDANT MERCY

God is a God of abundance.

His mercy is unfettered by time, material, or any other limitation. No sin is too deep for His mercy to forgive; no person is too lost for His mercy to find; no problem is too immense for His mercy to solve.

DAY 21

The Empty Cross

*For Christ sent me not to baptize,
but to preach the gospel: not with wisdom of
words, lest the cross of Christ should be made
of none effect. For the preaching of the cross
is to them that perish foolishness; but unto us
which are saved it is the power of God.*
—1 Corinthians 1:17–18

David Rose had worked at a garbage dump in the United Kingdom for fifteen years. He occasionally found interesting items and took them home. "I get to pull out whatever I like, mostly antiques," he told a British newspaper. One day in 2019 Rose found a few interesting items he thought might be valuable: a top hat, a box of cigars, and a stack of handwritten letters. Rose headed for London, where he took the items to be examined by experts on a television program devoted to rare antiques.

Appraisers examined the collection and determined that the items were authentic. The letters had been written by the personal cook of Sir Winston Churchill, who led Great Britain through World War II as prime minister. Churchill was known for wearing a top hat and smoking between eight and ten cigars each day. "She used to write to her son every day about the daily goings of Winston Churchill, what he was getting up to, how he was feeling, and just interesting stuff about him," Rose said.

The items were estimated to be worth $13,000. More importantly, the letters offered a new glimpse into the personal life of a great world leader, which historians will treasure for years to come. Yet for some reason the person who owned these items threw them into the trash. To value anything, one must first recognize its value. As the saying goes, one man's trash is another man's treasure.

There's a lesson there for followers of Jesus. The cross of Christ has inestimable worth. Through Christ's death and resurrection we have salvation from sin, fellowship with the Father, and the gift of eternal life. What treasure!

Yet to many this same cross has no value. They see it as a historical artifact at best and a myth at worst. Many in the ancient world considered it silly to think that God could die on a cross. Many in the modern world consider it nonsense that the dead can be raised to life. By dismissing the death and resurrection of Jesus as a fairy tale, they miss out on the great treasure of salvation. Only when we believe in the reality of the cross can we claim its power in our lives. It is by faith we are saved.

The cross represents both the best and worst moments in history. Jesus had to suffer and die so that we might live. Through His sacrifice we have new hope and new life. Through the cross Jesus redeemed His suffering and ours. Hold tightly to this truth. It has great power for those who believe.

MERCY PRINCIPLE

The cross of Jesus Christ has power,
but only for those who believe.

MERCY IN ACTION

Reflect *on what God has taught you today.*
I know

Express *your commitment, desire, or request to the Lord.*
I pray

Identify a *simple act of obedience God has prompted*
for you today.
I will

DAY 22

Slaying Lions, Passing Out Honey

But he told not them that he had taken the
honey out of the carcase of the lion.
—Judges 14:9

amson used his great strength to defeat a lion but
didn't dwell on the incident. Later, passing by the lion's
carcass, he discovered that bees had created a hive inside it. Samson retrieved the honey and shared the sweet
bounty with others, focusing on the joy of victory rather
than the fierce battle that preceded it. This story illustrates
a mercy moment. Concentrating on the victory that awaits
is far more enriching than being preoccupied with the
troubles we currently face.

It is worth noting that Samson's encounter with the
lion wasn't a chance occurrence during a casual stroll.
Scripture narrates how the lion's roar pierced the air when
Samson ventured into Timnath's vineyards. Satan does
not trouble those wandering without purpose. However,

when you approach the "vineyards"—symbolizing imminent spiritual triumph—the enemy comes to call.

Reflect on your life's current phase. Are you on the cusp of entering the "vineyard," where significant blessings await? This could relate to your education, career, or personal relationships. Maybe you're close to overcoming a longstanding temptation. Such moments are prime for the enemy to attack. The lion roars most loudly when you're about to make meaningful progress or when you're poised for a substantial victory. Through the Holy Ghost you are reminded of God's unparalleled power, leading to remarkable outcomes. The power you embody through the baptism of the Holy Ghost exceeds anything this world has ever witnessed or comprehended. It is mightier than any obstacle, financial hardship, or physical affliction.

The enemy strives to hide this divine power from you, persuading you of your inability to overcome the roaring lion. Yet the strength of God within you pulsates with life and vitality. By invoking Jesus Christ's authority, you can defeat Satan.

As you draw nearer to the "vineyard," expect the enemy's roar to intensify. Resist being consumed by fear or doubt. Remember—Satan has already been defeated! The victory was secured at Calvary by the precious sacrifice of Jesus, ensuring your victory as well. Embrace God's name with confidence and claim the strength that is rightfully yours. Your victory awaits.

MERCY PRINCIPLE

Don't focus on the battle; keep your eyes on victory.

MERCY IN ACTION

Reflect *on what God has taught you today.*
I know

Express *your commitment, desire, or request to the Lord.*
I pray

Identify a *victory you desire to win.*
I will

DAY 23

The Prayer of Jabez

And Jabez called on the God of Israel,
saying, Oh that thou wouldest bless me indeed,
and enlarge my coast, and that thine hand
might be with me, and that thou wouldest keep
me from evil, that it may not grieve me! And
God granted him that which he requested.
—1 Chronicles 4:10

Jabez was not an extraordinary person, but he had an extraordinary vision. He aspired for more than the mundane existence that seemed his lot. Craving to achieve and be more, he sought God's blessing to fulfill this ambition. Amazingly, God granted that request, illustrating His willingness to respond to the earnest pleas of those seeking to expand their horizons for His kingdom.

Your aspirations might not mirror Jabez's exactly, but you likely yearn for an increase in God's blessings in your life and to extend those blessings to others. Presenting your grand vision to the Lord can profoundly impact your life, just as it did for Jabez.

Jabez overcame the stigma associated with his name, which means "sorrow." Imagine being burdened by that name! Your name follows you wherever you go and sometimes precedes you. Although not many of us bear names that carry shame, overcoming a tarnished reputation can be equally challenging. Past behaviors or misdeeds can linger in the minds of others. Aligning with God's purpose and seeking His best and highest for your life enables you to overcome a "bad name." By God's grace, transformation is possible, allowing you to emerge anew, distinct from your past self. This alignment not only changes your path but also alters others' perceptions of you.

Jabez transcended earthly limitations and came alive with eternal purpose. When we are born again, we wake up to the reality of who God is and what He is doing in the world. This awakening revitalizes our perception and we recognize divine truth for the first time. Envisioning ourselves through God's eyes opens up possibilities previously unimagined. What more can you envision for your life through God's grace?

Of course, Jabez's prayer wasn't merely for self-gain; it was a pursuit of God's purposes. His plea to be kept from evil shows a desire to align with God's will. How many of us pray that God would enlarge our territory with no intention of aligning our hearts with God's? The Father's mercies are reserved for those aligned with His purpose.

By allowing God to expand his spiritual capacity, Jabez experienced the manifestation of His blessings. Faith and internal adjustments enable us to comprehend what the Lord desires to accomplish within us. Without divine intervention, our capacity to receive would remain limited.

Understanding God's nature, capabilities, and role in our lives empowers us to approach Him with the utmost confidence. He can pour out blessings upon us that we cannot contain. As our vision and perspective broaden, so should our readiness to embrace the growth God intends for us.

MERCY PRINCIPLE

*God pours out blessings on those who
have the capacity to receive them.*

MERCY IN ACTION

Reflect *on the changes required within you to embrace a
grander vision.*
I know

Express *the specific area in which you seek God's guidance
to enlarge your vision.*
I pray

Identify *how you will prepare for God's expanded opportunities within His kingdom.*
I will

DAY 24

What Is Your Source of Power?

And when the tempter came to him,
he said, If thou be the Son of God, command
that these stones be made bread. But he
answered and said, It is written, Man shall not
live by bread alone, but by every word that
proceedeth out of the mouth of God.
—Matthew 4:3–4

Satan employed every tactic to persuade Jesus to relinquish His identity, urging Him to forfeit the divine endowments granted by God: His power, His connection to the Father, and His divine mission. The tempter sought to divert Jesus from His true source of power, from His commitment to worshiping the one true God, and from enduring the suffering that would culminate in triumph according to God's ordained plan.

Our temptations may vary in form but their core intent remains consistent. Satan aims for us to relinquish the gifts

God has endowed, tempting us to trade eternal treasures for fleeting pleasures. God promises the abundant riches of His grace, active involvement in His purpose, and empowerment for a transformed life. We are called to be salt and light for the advancement of His kingdom, and God equips us with the strength to endure the trials unique to a Christian's journey.

This path, while leading to victory, invariably involves suffering—a prime moment for Satan's interventions. Temptations often masquerade as easier alternatives to God's high calling, sidelining the demanding task of purifying our hearts in exchange for fleeting comforts. It is far easier to attend a worship celebration and outwardly conform to piety than to engage in the profound, often arduous commitment to genuine transformation. Following Him feels effortless when life seems pleasant and God's blessings are obvious. Yet as we're faced with choices between personal gain and kingdom advancement, the tempter's allure becomes significantly compelling.

At some point in our journey, following Christ will lead to difficult choices—but we must resolve to partake in Christ's suffering so we may also experience His resurrection. Visualizing ourselves at the foot of the cross and witnessing Christ's precious blood flowing from His side fortifies our resolve to resist the simplistic temptations of Satan. Jesus suffered to fulfill the Father's will, providing a source of strength for His followers. His ordeal purifies us, converting our sinful inclinations into sanctified desires. Isaiah reminds us, "Though your sins be as scarlet, they shall be as white as snow" (Isaiah 1:18).

Furthermore, Christ's blood preserves us in the faith. Under the sprinkled blood, we are protected from the destroyer. The same blood that justifies us by removing sin also sanctifies us, invigorating our new nature and empowering us to overcome sin and faithfully follow God's commands. It sustains our perseverance in the faith. As it is written, "They overcame him by the blood of the Lamb" (Revelation 12:11).

Jesus triumphed through His suffering. His blood justifies, cleanses, and empowers us today. Remember the cross. Meditate on His suffering. Live empowered by His sacrificial blood, armed against temptation.

MERCY PRINCIPLE

Through Jesus's endurance of suffering,
we find our strength to persevere.

MERCY IN ACTION

Reflect *on what God has taught you today about the power of Christ's blood.*
I know

Express *to the Lord how you intend to confront the temptations in your life.*
I pray

Identify *a simple act of obedience to demonstrate your commitment to His will today.*
I will

DAY 25

Unlimited Grace

Unto an hundred talents of silver,
and to an hundred measures of wheat,
and to an hundred baths of wine,
and to an hundred baths of oil, and salt
without prescribing how much.
—Ezra 7:22

Salt has a number of uses. It can be used to preserve meat. It can also be used to add flavor to food. And it can tighten the gluten in wheat flour, making it rise more slowly and retain a firmer texture. Those living in colder climates know salt can also melt ice on roads, sidewalks, and parking lots. This plentiful and inexpensive compound is a miracle substance!

When God commanded that salt be used in every offering made to the Lord, He had several characteristics of salt in mind. First, salt preserves and purifies, symbolizing God's grace at work in us. As Thomas Watson said, "The salt of grace keeps the soul from putrefaction. Where there is the salt of grace, corruption does not breed. Though sin is in the heart, it does not reign. Grace is a bridle to check sin and a bit to hold it in."

The gift of salt by the Persian king Artaxerxes to Ezra the priest had no limit to the quantity, symbolizing abundance. This mirrors the limitless grace available in Jesus Christ. For those who seek it, grace is perpetually accessible, a crucial reminder during life's challenges. Our personal resources may be finite, but God's grace is inexhaustible, providing all we need.

And that's not all. Jesus described us as "the salt of the earth" (Matthew 5:13), indicating that just as grace preserves and purifies us, our presence in the world preserves us and those around us. We are the salt of the earth when we forgive others. We are salt when we counsel others and hold them accountable, preserving them from sin. We are salt when we melt the ice between enemies, helping them to become friends. The world around us should be a better place because we are here—purer, less cold, more temperate, and yes, more flavorful!

Unlike life's trials and sufferings, God's grace knows no bounds. We can confidently request what we need and we are assured it will be granted. This infinite resource enriches our lives, enabling us to confront challenges with joy, preserve our spirit, overcome sin, and reach our fullest potential, all while adding value to those around us.

MERCY PRINCIPLE

There is no limit to God's grace.

MERCY IN ACTION

Reflect *on what God has taught you today.*
I know

Express *your commitment, desire, or request to the Lord.*
I pray

Identify *a way you will act as "salt" to someone today.*
I will

DAY 26

The Quiet Realm

And my people shall dwell in
a peaceable habitation, and in sure dwellings,
and in quiet resting places."
—Isaiah 32:18

Living on earth is like staying at a cheap motel—dirty, dangerous, and very, very loud. This world is not a place of rest and peace. It's more often a place of danger, discomfort, and anxiety. Yet true peace and rest are not dictated by our surroundings or circumstances but are gifts from God to His children, available to all who seek Him.

Those unfamiliar with God's presence—people engrossed in worldly concerns—cannot know the peace and rest that come from knowing Him. How could they, when their minds and hearts are consumed with the world around them? This tranquility is a treasure exclusive to God's followers, bestowed by the Prince of Peace Himself.

When the death angel claimed the lives of Egypt's first-born, the blood protected God's chosen people. On their journey through the wilderness, a pillar of cloud protected them, and the rock gave them water to drink. While Israel traveled through the wilderness, God secured a resting place for the ark. God provides moments of rest for us in our journey.

Our refuge in chaos is found in the unshakable promises of our trustworthy God. His Word offers a sanctuary, a testament to His fidelity and the foundation of our peace. This peace, unaffected by external turmoil, is rooted in a profound trust and knowledge of God.

This divine peace is nurtured through our relationship with Jesus. Through communion, Scripture study, prayer, and worship, we invite His peace into our hearts. A lack of peace—being unsettled in spirit, anxious, or afraid—signals that we need to seek the Lord to reassess our obedience, confront any sin, and embrace repentance. Disobedience and dwelling on the past disrupt our inner peace.

Accepting God's grace means it is time to turn the page, leaving behind former ways and at times, relationships that contradict our commitment to Christ. We align ourselves with His peace by focusing our lives on Jesus and envisaging a future in His company.

To dwell in this peace, immerse yourself in His Word, engage in prayer, and seek moments of quiet reflection. Center your being in Christ. In His presence you will find peace.

MERCY PRINCIPLE

A heart centered on God will be at peace.

MERCY IN ACTION

Reflect *on what God has taught you today.*
I know

Express *your commitment, desire, or request to the Lord.*
I pray

Identify *an action to center your mind and heart on Jesus.*
I will

DAY 27

A Handful of Corn

There shall be a handful of corn in the earth
upon the top of the mountains; the fruit thereof
shall shake like Lebanon: and they of the city
shall flourish like grass of the earth.
—Psalm 72:16

In the agricultural heartlands vast expanses of land are dedicated to monocultures like wheat, corn, or soybeans. Farmers practice crop rotation to prevent soil depletion, so this year's wheat field might have hosted soybeans or corn in prior years.

From time to time you might spot a crop that seems out of place—for example, a solitary cornstalk towering above soybeans or even a few corn sprouts emerging from a roadside ditch or crack in an infrequently traveled country road. Farmers call these intrepid sprouts "volunteers." When corn is harvested, some kernels inevitably fall to the ground or get swept away by a gust of wind. If they land in fertile ground, even a tiny crack or crevice, they do what seeds do—they grow.

Though seemingly misplaced, these volunteer sprouts serve as reminders that growth and renewal are perennial forces in God's creation. A seed, even when dormant, retains life within.

David reflected a similar sentiment in his prayer for Solomon's kingship, asserting that God's purposes are ultimately fulfilled, even if it takes time. The repetitive use of the word *shall* emphasizes the certainty of the blessings that awaited Solomon and his kingdom. David's metaphor of a single corn ear flourishing atop a mountain symbolizes growth against the odds, illustrating how faith can cultivate abundance in the most improbable settings.

David pictured Solomon's reign as encompassing three pivotal roles. First, David said that Solomon would "save the children." Nurturing and protecting the vulnerable and innocent remains a vital mission for God's people. As we extend our love and care to the young, we sow seeds of hope that will bear fruit for generations to come.

Second, Solomon would also "break in pieces the oppressor." We too should stand against injustice and tyranny. We are empowered to challenge the status quo, dismantle oppressive systems, and advocate for the oppressed. Like Solomon, we become agents for transformation.

Last, the king's task included "delivering the needy." Our acts of kindness, no matter how small, can have a significant effect, touching the lives of others in ways we may not fully know. Just as the handful of meal in the widow's barrel never ran out, our generosity and compassion can lead to abundant blessings for us and those we serve. This image of fruitful ministry should inspire us to take similar action.

So when you notice a plant thriving against the odds, let it inspire you. Like the volunteer cornstalk, you can yield a fruitful harvest in your sphere, regardless of the circumstances.

MERCY PRINCIPLE

The power of God can transform even the most unlikely people and places.

MERCY IN ACTION

Reflect *on what God has taught you today.*
I know

Express *your commitment, desire, or request to the Lord.*
I pray

Identify a *simple act of obedience God has prompted for you today.*
I will

DAY 28

There Is a Place by Me

*And the Lord said, Behold, there is a place by
me, and thou shalt stand upon a rock.*
—Exodus 33:21

At 11:30 a.m. on May 29, 1953, Edmund Hillary, a New Zealander formerly engaged in beekeeping, completed a 29,035-foot climb to become the first person confirmed to have reached the summit of Mount Everest, the world's tallest peak. Many before him had attempted this daunting climb, with at least two adventurers losing their lives in the process. However, Hillary's discovery of a narrow crevice in a rock face, which he painstakingly navigated to reach the top, marked his success.

While Edmund Hillary's name is celebrated worldwide, the name of Tenzing Norgay, the Nepalese Sherpa who accompanied Hillary, often receives less recognition. Yet Norgay played a crucial role in the climb. The duo braved the night at nearly 28,000 feet, relying on bottled oxygen to breathe in the thin air. On the morning that followed, their continued ascent led to Hillary's historic summit. Hillary then extended a rope to assist Norgay in joining him, and together they stood at the world's highest point.

The act of climbing mountains, whether as a physical challenge or a spiritual quest, is not meant to be undertaken alone. God calls us to venture into His kingdom, assuring us of His presence. He doesn't expect us to reach new heights by ourselves; instead, He guides us every step of the way. As we draw near to the peak, He offers His hand, inviting us to stand with Him in the place He has already secured for us. God's divine plan encompasses a specific place for each of us, a destination prepared with our journey in mind.

If you find yourself in a period of confusion, searching for your designated place within God's grand design, the journey ahead may appear formidable. The heights He calls you to may seem beyond your reach. It's crucial to remember that God is already there at every destination He calls you to explore. He has prepared the path and ensured a place for you to stand firmly. This journey, while personal and unique to each of us, is also a shared experience, reminding us of the collective ascent we undertake in faith, guided by the hand of God and supported by the fellowship of those who journey alongside us.

MERCY PRINCIPLE

The place the Lord leads is unknown to us—but not to Him.

MERCY IN ACTION

Reflect *on what God has taught you today.*
I know

Express *your commitment, desire, or request to the Lord.*
I pray

Identify a *simple act of obedience God has prompted for you today.*
I will

DAY 29

I Have Come for Your Words

Death and life are in the power of the tongue:
and they that love it shall eat the fruit thereof.
—Proverbs 18:21

Scientists have devoted countless hours to studying the origins of the universe. The prevailing theory is the big bang, which posits that all matter exploded outward from a singular point. While this may be scientifically supported, Scripture provides a more straightforward account: God spoke, and it was so. The world was created by the simple act of speech. There is power in God's words.

In a more modest sense, our words also wield significant power. The things we say can profoundly affect ourselves, others, and even the broader world for better or worse. Our words can shape our reality. Aligning our words with God's promises can lead to incredible outcomes. Speaking carelessly can unleash great harm.

You have probably noticed this in relation to the words of others. A compliment can buoy our spirits, whereas even a mild insult can trigger feelings of anger or sadness. Your parents likely shaped your view of the world and yourself through words spoken to or about you. Their words had power. Your words have power too.

Consider the self-talk after a making a mistake, missing an appointment, or succumbing to temptation. Many resort to self-condemnation: "I'm so stupid!" "I hate myself!" "I can't do anything right!" Such declarations are not only false; they also diverge sharply from God's view of us. Yet if we repeat these statements, they begin feeling true, shaping our self-perception and future behavior. Our words have power, even over our own minds.

Rather than unleashing destruction on yourself or others through your words, why not unleash the power of God? Reflect on what God says about you and His vision for your life, family, and community. Unleash divine power by speaking that to yourself and others.

I am a child of God. I am forgiven, loved, and free. God has an eternal plan for my life. No plan of the enemy formed against me can succeed. I can do all things through Christ, who gives me strength. I am growing in the Spirit day by day. Tomorrow will be better than today.

While we must confront our setbacks and failings, remember that in moments of sin, we have an advocate in Jesus, who intercedes for us with the Father. Confession brings forgiveness, accessible through faith in Christ.

Dwelling on failure has no benefit. Accusations stem from Satan, whereas Jesus stands as our defender. Avoid being your own accuser. Instead, speak to yourself and others with grace, compassion, kindness, and hope, echoing the words of Jesus.

MERCY PRINCIPLE

Your words have power. Use that power for good.

MERCY IN ACTION

Reflect *on what God has taught you today.*
I know

Express *your commitment, desire, or request to the Lord.*
I pray

Identify a *simple act of obedience God has prompted for you today.*
I will

DAY 30

Put the Sacrifice in Order

*And he put the wood in order, and cut the
bullock in pieces, and laid him on the wood,
and said, Fill four barrels with water, and pour
it on the burnt sacrifice, and on the wood.*
—1 Kings 18:33

Product engineers have coined a term for designs so straightforward that anyone can use them without difficulty: *idiot-proof*. We've all benefited from products designed with simplicity in mind.

Consider the nine-volt battery, distinguished by uniquely shaped terminals that prevent incorrect insertion. Similarly, electronic memory cards feature a notched corner, ensuring that they cannot be inserted upside down into devices like cameras or cell phones. Such design decisions highlight a fundamental principle: when there is only one correct method to perform an action, a skilled designer will ensure that it is the only possible way.

Despite these precautions, there is no guarantee some stubborn consumer won't try to force the batteries in the wrong way or jam the memory card into the slot backward, convinced of his or her method's correctness. As one engineer humorously noted, just when you think a problem has been solved—along comes a bigger idiot!

The ultimate designer, of course, is God. He designed the world with specific operational guidelines, providing clear instructions for its optimal use. This is exemplified in the passage above, 1 Kings 18:33. God gave Elijah careful instructions for this sacrifice, right down to how the wood should be arranged. Elijah followed those instructions perfectly, and the result was spectacular.

When we surrender entirely to God's will, we align ourselves more perfectly with His intentions. Adhering to His guidance as closely as we can enables us to accomplish great things according to His perfect plan. Navigating through God's world is far less arduous when we follow His instructions.

This adherence includes following the dictates of Scripture, of course. Yet because God knew that some of us like to put the battery in backward, he also released the Holy Ghost to us. Our connection with God through the Spirit unlocks the unique, divinely intended design for our lives. Faithfully follow God's lead. Don't look for shortcuts or arrogantly believe you can design a better system for your life. Trust God and allow Him to guide you each step of the way.

MERCY PRINCIPLE

God's way is the only right way.

MERCY IN ACTION

Reflect *on what God has taught you today.*
I know

Express *your commitment, desire, or request to the Lord.*
I pray

Identify a *simple act of obedience God has prompted for you today.*
I will

ENDURING MERCY

*God's mercy is unwavering and accessible
in every circumstance.*

No situation can sever the bond of God's mercy—from the confines of a prison to the comfort of your home. His mercy meets your material and spiritual needs. Your relationship with God is the most durable relationship in your life.

DAY 31

The Blessing Will Overtake You

And all these blessings shall come on thee,
and overtake thee, if thou shalt hearken
unto the voice of the Lord thy God.
—Deuteronomy 28:2

God's blessings do not require a chase; they will find you. God established a spiritual precedent in the sacred covenant with Israel that would shape the kingdom's essence and guide generations toward His rich promises. Intriguingly, He called His beloved people to take the first step of obedience, which initiated blessings—and we must do the same. We are tasked with igniting the process of obedience. The blessings of God have always followed those who walk faithfully in His ways. This commitment to divine order allows our character to flourish as we increasingly possess His magnificent promises.

The Bible assures us that God's blessings will overtake us as we work toward obedience. Have you fully surrendered to God? Consider how many unclaimed blessings await your complete submission.

By deepening our faith and obedience, attentively listening with our hearts to God's whispers and taking action, we unlock an abundance of blessings. The gift of God's mercy hastens to catch up with us as we walk steadfastly along the course ordained by the Lord. Conversely, when we disregard His voice, we cannot hope to outrun the troubles that occur or elude the consequences of our disobedience.

Blessings ardently pursue those who engage in the sacred dance of obedience. Scripture affirms, "Draw nigh to God, and he will draw nigh to you" (James 4:8). David proclaimed, "Surely goodness and mercy shall follow me" (Psalm 23:6), while Jesus promised the disciples, "These signs shall follow them that believe" (Mark 16:17). Our actions trigger God's blessing.

Deuteronomy 28 reveals a nuanced understanding of obedience and blessings. The people refrained from affirming the blessings with "Amen" because they understood that receiving them required more than simple agreement; it required obedience. Conversely, they acknowledged the curses with "Amen" because they understood it would take an act of defiance to activate the curse. The blessing is automatic when we obey. The curse is activated when we disobey. To inherit God's blessings, all that was required of the people was to listen to His voice and walk the path laid out for them.

God has untold blessings stored up for you. You cannot claim those blessings by running away from God. And you cannot outrun those blessings when you submit yourself to God. You have a decision to make: Will you move toward God, guided by the Holy Ghost? Or will you follow your own will and desires?

MERCY PRINCIPLE

Blessings overtake us on the path of obedience.

MERCY IN ACTION

Reflect *on what God has taught you today.*
I know

Express *your commitment, desire, or request to the Lord.*
I pray

Identify a *simple act of obedience God has prompted for you today.*
I will

DAY 32

Back to the King's Gate

And Mordecai came again to the king's gate.
But Haman hasted to his house mourning,
and having his head covered.
—Esther 6:12

Victory may arrive suddenly but its foundation is laid gradually, day by day. At the age of nineteen I attended a banquet for evangelists featuring some of the era's most renowned speakers. Their presence and awe-inspiring messages stirred a deep yearning within my soul to preach the gospel effectively. Yet I left that event under a cloud of discouragement. I recognized the vast chasm between the towering stature of these great men and my own humble beginnings. This wasn't self-pity but a sober acknowledgment of my journey ahead. In the presence of these great evangelists, my own shortcomings became painfully obvious. I was filled with self-doubt.

Instead of succumbing to despair, however, I turned to my lifelong practice of seeking the Lord's guidance through prayer and fasting. On the fifth day of a grueling fast, my strength waning, I earnestly prayed for direction. I said, "God, I don't know how to do this. I'm not going to make it." That night God's voice awakened me with a clear message: "Brian, seek me daily and I will reveal the way."

The Spirit led me to the ancient tale of Esther and Mordecai. Mordecai's daily presence at the king's gate, his humility, and his critical role in thwarting a plot against the king reveal the power of steadfast obedience (see Esther 6:1–11). Even after receiving a parade in honor of his role in saving the king's life, Mordecai returned to his prayer vigil at the king's gate, sitting in sackcloth and ashes because of a conspiracy against the Jewish people—a testament to his unwavering commitment.

Inspired by Mordecai, I adopted the "Rule of Five"—a sacred code that has profoundly impacted my entire life and ministry. Although John C. Maxwell coined the term, the principle has been a cornerstone of my spiritual practice for years.

My Rule of Five includes the following:

1. Engaging deeply with the Word through reading, study, and prayer

2. Writing and teaching from my learnings

3. Offering vision and encouragement to another leader

4. Speaking the Word to a heart in need

5. Reflecting on the day's events

Adhering to these practices, much like Mordecai's fidelity to the king's gate, has brought God's mercy into my life in triumphs and trials alike. Your Rule of Five may vary from mine, but establishing daily spiritual habits is crucial for enduring life's fluctuations. When the enemy attacks, let him find you steadfast, always seeking the Lord at "the King's gate."

MERCY PRINCIPLE

Consistent daily spiritual practices
foster personal obedience.

MERCY IN ACTION

Reflect *on what God has taught you today.*
I know

Express *your commitment, desire, or request to the Lord.*
I pray

Identify a *simple act of obedience God has prompted*
for you today.
I will

DAY 33

They Will Seek Me Early

*I will go and return to my place, till they
acknowledge their offence, and seek my face:
in their affliction they will seek me early.*
—Hosea 5:15

Adversity, though unpleasant, serves as the faithful Shepherd's guiding hand, leading His wandering sheep back to the fold. Like diligent sheepdogs, life's trials nudge at our heels, gently directing us toward the safety of the Father's embrace. Paradoxically, our abundance often necessitates this guidance. Overindulgence in God's gifts can lead to forgetfulness of His presence, emphasizing the importance of daily seeking His face.

Remember these words of David: "And in my prosperity I said, I shall never be moved" (Psalm 30:6). David's experience, feeling unshakable in prosperity yet humbled by adversity, mirrors our own. When adversity and hardship weigh heavily upon us, we discover the same lesson David learned. "Before I was afflicted I went astray: but now have

I kept thy word" (Psalm 119:67). Hardships remind us of our dependence on God, propelling us toward His salvation and sustenance. Approaching God with open hands allows us to fully receive His blessings. This open hand makes it possible for us to know God and to never lose our joy in His presence.

Recognizing His discipline in our struggles helps us see our true state, much like the prodigal son, who sought not his father's *house* but his *father* himself, understanding his need for reconciliation and relying on his father's goodness. Again, the prodigal son did not say he would return to his father's *house*. He said, "I will arise and go to my father" (Luke 15:18). This distinction is profound. He did not seek the comfort and security of his father's house but rather the presence of his father—the source of those blessings. The son realized his misdeeds had cost him his rightful place in the family. His path to redemption wasn't through reclaiming his lost inheritance but rather in seeking the compassionate embrace of his father, trusting in his father's inherent goodness. Stripped of the privileges he had squandered, the son relied solely on his father's merciful nature for restoration.

In times of trial, consider these times as an opportunity to refocus on God rather than your situation or worldly comforts. Let adversity strip away self-reliance, turning your heart fully to God's enduring love, which triumphs over all hardships.

MERCY PRINCIPLE

Adversity compels believers to return to our loving Father.

MERCY IN ACTION

Reflect *on what God has taught you today.*
I know

Express *your commitment, desire, or request to the Lord.*
I pray

Identify *one action today to rely on God rather than posses-sions or people.*
I will

DAY 34

Say unto This Mountain

And Jesus said unto them,
Because of your unbelief: for verily I say unto
you, If ye have faith as a grain of mustard seed,
ye shall say unto this mountain, Remove hence
to yonder place; and it shall remove;
and nothing shall be impossible unto you.
—Matthew 17:20

Whales are the largest of God's creatures and the unchallenged masters of the sea. The Antarctic blue whale, stretching nearly one hundred feet and weighing over 400,000 pounds, is a testament to this magnificence. Yet, despite their dominance, whales can find themselves in danger due to inattention.

A telling headline about beached whales in California encapsulates this tragedy— "Giants Perish while Chasing Minnows." Focused on pursuing minor prey, these majestic beings neglected their environment, ultimately stranding themselves as the tide retreated.

This scenario mirrors how we often squander our potential, preoccupied with the insignificant at the expense of embracing our rightful stature as God's children. It is a mistake that is certainly easy to make. Think of the disciples who lived in the presence of Jesus every day. They were not only elected by Jesus to continue His mission but also qualified, having performed miraculous healings, exorcisms, and powerful preaching. Yet, they all succumbed to human frailty and scattered in the Garden of Gethsemane, leaving their Lord to face arrest alone. Peter denied knowing Jesus to avoid trouble with the authorities. Judas, who must have known Christ as well as the rest, even chose to betray him. Whether it is the desire to save our reputation, our skin, or gain a few more pieces of silver, we can all fall into the trap of losing ourselves by chasing something trivial.

Avoiding such pitfalls requires maintaining our connection to God's anointing. We stay pointed in the right direction by speaking about what we desire to see and refusing to let circumstances dictate our words. Our words play a crucial role in shaping our reality. They shape our thoughts, direct our paths, and influence our actions. Speaking with faith fosters strength; succumbing to defeat or negativity leads us astray. Proverbs 18:21 underscores this: "Death and life are in the power of the tongue: and they that love it shall eat the fruit thereof."

Fortunately, even the faintest whisper of faith can overpower the loudest cries of despair. A mere speck of faith grants us immense authority within God's kingdom.

God has granted us the power to speak with inner peace, emboldened by our divine mission. Our chosen words wield immense power, capable of orchestrating order and manifesting God's kingdom amidst chaos.

MERCY PRINCIPLE

Your words wield significant power in your life.

MERCY IN ACTION

Reflect *on what God has taught you today.*
I know

Express *your commitment, desire, or request to the Lord.*
I pray

Identify *your faith-driven motto for today.*
I will

DAY 35

The Need for a Personal Revival

Though I walk in the midst of trouble,
thou wilt revive me: thou shalt stretch forth
thine hand against the wrath of mine enemies,
and thy right hand shall save me.
—Psalm 138:7

Have you ever felt lost amidst life's relentless pace, stressed by deadlines, weighed down by expectations, or defeated by daily responsibilities? The cycle of busyness and stress is daunting and hard to escape, leading to exhaustion and a sense of defeat.

It starts with taking on responsibilities or challenges that initially energize us—things like becoming parents and taking on new work projects—which can initially give a sense of growth and importance. Before long, however, the excitement gives way to stress, possibly due to conflicts at work or home, criticism, or financial strain. What once felt fulfilling now seems suffocating, affecting our relationships, health, and well-being. Yet even in these low moments, reminiscent of "the valley of the shadow of death" David describes in Psalm 23, there is hope.

In our darkest times God will revive our spirits. Amidst seemingly insurmountable problems, God is present. We are never alone. He is always ready to refresh our spirits, offering the strength we need to face life's trials. God's presence is unwavering. He walks beside us during difficult times, offering support against stress, conflict, fatigue, and illness. Guided by His wisdom and led by His Spirit, we can surmount any obstacle. Our victories are gifts from the Lord, not the result of our strength alone.

When we seek God, we will find Him and experience the power of personal revival. God awaits to restore and refresh our spirits, providing strength, courage, and direction. However, this renewal requires our active pursuit. Instead of resorting to unhealthy coping mechanisms— like overeating, resorting to alcohol, or other self-indulgent behavior—we should seek God through prayer and engagement with scripture, opening our hearts to His guidance.

Revival is a process, not an instant remedy. If you're caught in a downward spiral, remember that it took time to reach this point, and recovery will also require patience and persistence. It takes time for your body to rest. It takes time for your mind to be healed. It takes time for your spirit to gain strength. Seek the Lord and keep seeking. Personal revival is not a quick fix—it's a way of life.

MERCY PRINCIPLE

God renews those who earnestly seek Him.

MERCY IN ACTION

Reflect *on what God has taught you today about your current condition—physically, mentally, and spiritually.*
I know

Express *your commitment, desire, or request to the Lord.*
I pray

Identify *how you will pursue God's presence today.*
I will

DAY 36

The Inner Struggle

*That he would grant you, according to
the riches of his glory, to be strengthened with
might by his Spirit in the inner man; That Christ
may dwell in your hearts by faith.*
—Ephesians 3:16–17

Michael Phelps, the most decorated Olympic athlete in history, secured twenty-eight swimming medals, setting a record for gold medals in individual events. Phelps defeated all of the most prominent competitors in the world. Interestingly, his training for the sport and pre-competition ritual had nothing to do with the competition. Phelps's focus was on winning the greatest battle any athlete will face—the battle that takes place in the mind.

Before each event, Phelps entered the natatorium with a singular focus. He did not look at competitors or the pool's details. He often wore a hoodie, earbuds in place, head down, eyes closed—not in avoidance but in deep concentration. He visualized every aspect of his race: the dive, each stroke, the turns, and the final push to victory. For Phelps, victory was first achieved in the mind.

This principle applies equally to followers of Christ. Spiritual battles are waged and won in the mind before any worldly triumph. As believers progress spiritually or in ministry, they encounter new challenges and heightened opposition. Success in these arenas demands inner strength to overcome adversities, including intensified attacks, temptations, and setbacks. The real contest is spiritual.

Self-doubt is perhaps the most formidable enemy for a servant of God, eroding faith and undermining spiritual authority. Introducing self-doubt into ministry cripples our ability to wield spiritual power effectively, impacting our work for God. Too often we try to address this lack of confidence by learning some new method or technique. However, the solution lies not in external strategies but in bolstering spiritual authority through internal spiritual development. And that can come only through an inner, spiritual process. Overcoming doubt, renewing faith, strengthening convictions, and steadfast adherence to God's Word enhances spiritual authority, empowering believers to fulfill their divine calling confidently.

Leading athletes must mentally fortify themselves before their physical endeavors. Similarly, even the most devout saints have faced doubts and fears. However, they did not allow these inner conflicts to define them or hinder their impact. Instead, they persevered, seeking God's strength and guidance to overcome their struggles. Embrace the battles within, for they are opportunities for growth and transformation.

MERCY PRINCIPLE

Inner victory must precede effective ministry.

MERCY IN ACTION

Reflect *on what God has taught you today.*
I know

Express *your commitment, desire, or request to the Lord.*
I pray

Identify a *simple act of obedience God has prompted for you today.*
I will

DAY 37

The Exceeding Greatness of His Power

*And what is the exceeding greatness of
his power to us-ward who believe, according
to the working of his mighty power.*
—Ephesians 1:19

Those living near one of the Great Lakes are used to snowfall. Yet the patterns of snowfall can be unpredictable. When weather conditions are just right, "snow bands" form over these large bodies of water, producing heavy but intermittent snowfall. Snow bands are like streams of clouds that gather moisture over water and then dump it in the form of snow when reaching land. These long, finger-like bands oscillate back and forth like radio waves. A snow band may drop six inches of snow, then drift a bit to the north. For an hour or so the snow stops, the sky is clear, and the sun shines. But longtime residents won't be fooled. They know the band will soon drift southward again, bringing several more inches of snow.

This can happen several times over a day or two, dropping several feet of snow. Just when you think it's over, it starts again.

Our inheritance in Jesus Christ, like these bands of snow, is inexhaustible. Just when you think you have received all God has for His saints, He reveals even more. This is the message Paul so urgently communicated to the Ephesian church. God's gift to you exceeds whatever small taste you have experienced so far. No matter how richly God has blessed you, there is more power, more blessings, and more inheritance coming. Christ's forgiveness of sins, adoption, acceptance, and deliverance constitute a great inheritance, so great that we can scarcely comprehend it.

God created the world, and He exceeded that by creating humankind. God established the nation of Israel, but He exceeded that by sending Jesus Christ. God has saved you from sin, but He exceeds that by making you holy. God has declared you His child, but He will exceed that by giving you eternal life.

Regardless of what happens today or tomorrow, no matter your circumstances, doubts, or trials, know this—the exceeding greatness of God's power in us surpasses it all.

MERCY PRINCIPLE

*However great you believe
God's power to be, it is greater still.*

MERCY IN ACTION

Reflect *on what God has taught you today.*
I know

Express *your commitment, desire, or request to the Lord.*
I pray

Identify a *simple act of obedience God has prompted
for you today.*
I will

DAY 38

Guard the Altar

*And two parts of all you that go
forth on the sabbath, even they shall keep the
watch of the house of the Lord about the king.
And ye shall compass the king round about, every
man with his weapons in his hand: and he that cometh
within the ranges, let him be slain: and be ye with the
king as he goeth out and as he cometh in. And the
captains over the hundreds did according to all things
that Jehoiada the priest commanded: and they took
every man his men that were to come in on the sabbath,
with them that should go out on the sabbath, and
came to Jehoiada, the priest. And to the captains
over hundreds did the priest give king David's spears
and shields, that were in the temple of the Lord.
And the guard stood, every man with his weapons
in his hand, round about the king, from the right corner
of the temple to the left corner of the temple, along
by the altar and the temple. And he brought forth
the king's son, and put the crown upon him,*

and gave him the testimony;
they made him king, and anointed him;
they clapped their hands, and said,
God save the king.
— 2 Kings 11:7–12

Dark times had descended upon the land of Judah. The government was rampant with corruption and the widespread worship of foreign gods. The young King Azariah's death, just a year into his reign, precipitated a crisis. His mother, Athaliah, daughter of the notorious King Ahab and Queen Jezebel of Israel, seized the throne and sought to eliminate all royal family members to consolidate her power. Only one life stood between Athaliah and absolute power: the infant Joash, Azariah's son and the sole surviving heir of David's royal lineage.

In this critical moment Jehoiada, the high priest, emerged as a protector. He concealed the young heir within the temple's sanctuary, safeguarding him from Athaliah's murderous intent for seven years. Eventually Joash was crowned king, restoring his father's legacy. Athaliah's reign of terror ended with her execution, and the nation witnessed the revival of true worship of God.

This narrative is a testament to hope's endurance, even amidst the deepest shadows of uncertainty. God's presence and purpose persist through the darkest periods, guiding history toward His ultimate design. This truth, evident in Joash's era, remains relevant in our contemporary world of challenges.

We live in uncertain times. International threats imperil the fragile peace in our world. Our society, already altered by the prevalence of information technology, now grapples with the uncertainty produced by artificial intelligence and the manipulation of images and information. Each decade seems to bring a new and deadly disease or health crisis. Queen Athaliah may be long gone, but the enemy always has fresh troops at his disposal.

Yet God's will is eternal and His purpose cannot be defeated. We are never alone. There is always a remnant, a beacon of hope illuminating even the darkest times. As we face challenges and uncertainties, let us draw strength from the knowledge that God is working behind the scenes, protecting and preserving His purpose for us.

The coronation of the rightful king, Joash, and the jubilant proclamation of "God save the king" reminds us of the inexorable march of God's will. In our time we witness equivalent acts of valor. Brave souls still rise up to stand in the gap between good and evil. People of courage still speak the truth, shelter the helpless, feed the hungry, and work for justice. Inspired by the legacies of Jehoiada and Joash and the myriad instances of God's light piercing the darkness, we can face adversity with renewed resolve.

MERCY PRINCIPLE

A single point of light dispels the darkness.

MERCY IN ACTION

Reflect *on what God has taught you today.*
I know

Express *your commitment, desire, or request to the Lord.*
I pray

Identify a *simple act of obedience God has prompted for you today.*
I will

DAY 39

The Ministry of Waiting

And David went thence to Mizpeh of Moab:
and he said unto the king of Moab,
Let my father and my mother, I pray thee,
come forth, and be with you,
till I know what God will do for me.
—1 Samuel 22:3

David, the great poet-king of Israel, is one of history's most heroic figures. His bravery, courage, faith, and devotion were unparalleled. Yet David was not immune to errors, some of which exacted a high cost.

One significant low point in David's reign was when he was forced out of Jerusalem due to a rebellion led by his son Absalom. As a young man, David had endured great opposition and even death threats from King Saul. But those days were supposed to have been behind him as he settled into his kingly role, enjoying the power and respect it brought. His expulsion from Jerusalem, therefore, was not just a defeat but also a deep humiliation.

During his retreat, the once-exalted David faced humiliating taunts and curses from his enemies. Rather than striking back at those deriding him, David maintained his composure, entrusting his fate to God. He was prepared to accept whatever God willed—whether it was a restoration to power or a life of obscurity in the wilderness. This episode in David's life highlighted the futility of fighting his battles alone.

At some point every believer faces a moment like this one, arriving there through personal failings or the actions of others. We might lose honor, wealth, career opportunities, or marital harmony. Our temptation might be to lash out, become defensive, argue with critics, or attempt damage control, but such responses rarely yield spiritual growth or positive change.

David's example inspires us to embrace the unknown with faith and patience, leaving our future in God's hands and remaining open to His direction. It is in the ministry of waiting that we find solace in the perfection of God's counsel, whether it leads to restoration and blessings or challenges and banishment. There is a blessing in submitting to God's will, whatever it might be. In those moments we deepen our faith and mature spiritually.

In challenging times let us not rush to fight or flee but instead take time to discern God's purpose. Embrace a period of mourning and grief if necessary, but do so with the knowledge that God's plan is ever unfolding. Let's discover what the Lord will do for us. Submission to God provides the strength to overcome trials, and trusting His guidance will lead us to a future filled with hope and blessings.

MERCY PRINCIPLE

Wait upon God before engaging in battle.

MERCY IN ACTION

Reflect *on what God has taught you today.*
I know

Express *your commitment, desire, or request to the Lord.*
I pray

Identify a *simple act of obedience God has prompted for you today.*
I will

DAY 40

And These Are Ancient Things

*And Jokim, and the men of Chozeba,
and Joash, and Saraph, who had the
dominion in Moab, and Jashubilehem.
And these are ancient things.*
—1 Chronicles 4:22

Daily life is inherently repetitive. Each day introduces fresh problems and challenges, joys and sorrows, opportunities and setbacks. Navigating through each day often consumes most of our energy, making it easy to get caught up in the immediacy of our current circumstances.

Have you noticed how quickly cultural fads spread through our society? One day the latest celebrity, hit song, or fashion trend is unknown, and the next day it dominates public discourse. Every election is billed as the most crucial of all time. Every fluctuation in interest rates is framed as a harbinger of either prosperity or doom. We live not merely in the now but in the *right* now. While this can be thrilling, it more often proves exhausting and disheartening.

When life's immediate pressures lead to stress or uncertainty, it is beneficial to pause and reflect on things that are timeless rather than temporary. Our faith is not the invention of a social media account or a blip in the latest economic forecast. Our beliefs are ancient, rooted in eternity. We were chosen for salvation before the foundation of the world, selected through God's eternal love. The Father's love for you predates creation, extending through all eternity.

This ancient story continues unfolding. Your life is part of a grand narrative that stretches from before time began until after it ends. You play a role in God's eternal story and your life in Him will never end. Each day presents a fresh opportunity to create something extraordinary, to overcome challenges, and to inspire others through your actions. You possess the power to shape your destiny and leave a legacy that echoes throughout time, just as those who preceded us did.

God's eternal purpose in redeeming us from sin is to cleanse us, sanctify us, and glorify us. His intention remains constant and unchanging throughout time, as God's covenant with us is everlasting. Although the sun's daily cycle signifies the passage of time, the love that God has for his children is boundless and eternal, without beginning or end.

As you navigate life's unpredictable ups and downs, it is important to remember that each day is temporary, but God's promises endure forever. The same powerful forces that guided and empowered Jokim, Joash, and

Saraph to have dominion in a hostile environment also dwell within you. These ancient truths affirm the significance of your existence and the inherent potential for greatness. Spending time in God's presence will renew your spirit and give you the hope that as you connect to the ancient promises and pursue them, you will possess all that God has for you.

MERCY PRINCIPLE

God's love for you has no beginning and no end.

MERCY IN ACTION

Reflect *on what God has taught you today.*
I know

Express *your commitment, desire, or request to the Lord.*
I pray

Identify a *simple act of obedience God has prompted for you today.*
I will

ABOUT THE AUTHOR

BRIAN KINSEY is the senior pastor of First Pentecostal Church of Pensacola, Florida. He has a wealth of ministry experience, having served as an evangelist for many years, a pastor in Louisiana for five years, and in the headquarters of the United Pentecostal Church in St. Louis as youth president and as secretary of the North American Missions Division for the denomination.

Kinsey holds a Master of Arts in theology and has authored six books:

- *The Bride's Pearl: A Commentary on Ephesians*
- *Made for More: 7 Proven Strategies for Reaching Your Full Potential*
- *The Dancing Father: Discover Joy and Power through a Daily Relationship with God*
- *The Bride's Prize: A Commentary on Philippians*
- *I Choose to Win: How to Get Unstuck, On Track, and Enjoy Abundant Life*
- *Qualified for Your Anointing*

Kinsey is a noted speaker and has traveled extensively around the world in this capacity. He is passionate about developing the ministries of others. He provides leadership training through seminars, training sessions, and a mentoring program titled "Refresh: Training Leaders to Be Their Best," which can be accessed at *www.briankinsey.com*.

Pastor Kinsey and his wife, Lanette, have three children and six grandchildren.

www.ingramcontent.com/pod-product-compliance
Lightning Source LLC
LaVergne TN
LVHW051235080426
835513LV00016B/1600